MW00437307

Lent and Holy Week
WITH
Mary

Lent and Holy Week

with Mary

REFLECTIONS BY THE AFFILIATES OF MAYSLAKE MINISTRIES

Edited by Dr. Mary Amore

Our Sunday Visitor

www.osv.com
Our Sunday Visitor Publishing Division
Our Sunday Visitor, Inc.
Huntington, Indiana 46750

Scripture quotations are from the *Revised Standard Version of the Bible—Second Catholic Edition* (Ignatius Edition), copyright © 1965, 1966, 2006 National Council of the Churches of Christ in the United States of America. Used by permission. All rights reserved.

Every reasonable effort has been made to determine copyright holders of excerpted materials and to secure permissions as needed. If any copyrighted materials have been inadvertently used in this work without proper credit being given in one form or another, please notify Our Sunday Visitor in writing so that future printings of this work may be corrected accordingly.

Copyright © 2017 by Mayslake Ministries. Published 2017.

22 21 20 19 18 17   1 2 3 4 5 6 7 8 9

All rights reserved. With the exception of short excerpts for critical reviews, no part of this work may be reproduced or transmitted in any form or by any means whatsoever without permission from the publisher. For more information, visit: www.osv.com/permissions.

Our Sunday Visitor Publishing Division
Our Sunday Visitor, Inc.
200 Noll Plaza
Huntington, IN 46750
1-800-348-2440

ISBN: 978-1-68192-251-5 (Inventory No. X1946)
LCCN: 2017956925

Cover design: Tyler Ottinger
Cover art: Shutterstock
Interior design: Dianne Nelson

PRINTED IN THE UNITED STATES OF AMERICA

Reflections

Ash Wednesday: Self-Control

"Finally, brethren, whatever is true, whatever is honorable, whatever is just, whatever is pure, whatever is lovely, whatever is gracious, if there is any excellence, if there is anything worthy of praise, think about these things."
— *Philippians 4:8*

This letter from St. Paul offers us a blueprint of perfection for us to dwell upon. If we really study this text, the attributes perfectly describe someone who practices self-control — the ability to choose wisely over the things of this world.

These characteristics also describe our Blessed Mother. Mary is a model of truth; she is honorable and right, accepting the joys and sorrows of life, but always choosing a steadfast faith in God. Mary is pure and lovely and good. If there is anyone worthy of praise, it is Mary, the mother of Jesus.

We can follow the life of the Blessed Mother by living a life worthy of praise. In times of difficulty, Mary can help us practice self-control.

— Lauren Nelson

SPEND TIME TODAY dwelling on the attributes listed in this reading. Reflect on how Mary can assist you to dwell on these things.

Prayer: Mary, keep me in your most pure heart. You are wonderful and good; help me to follow your example.

Thursday After Ash Wednesday: Gentleness

*"O LORD, in the morning you hear my voice; /
in the morning I prepare a sacrifice for you, and watch."*
— *Psalm 5:3*

Daylight doesn't come at full force all at once. It grows gently on the horizon and then spreads across the sky. Here the words of the psalmist offer us a gentle reminder of the stillness of the dawn as we rise to greet a new day. As most of us know, however, life can also be noisy in the morning. Our pets are waiting to be fed, children need to get off to school, and we hurry to get ready for work. The household awakens and the sounds of the television and the hum of the computer can break the quiet, gentle space of morning at sunrise.

Like us, Mary's life also had its noisy moments. Still, Mary remained quietly devoted to God. She carried the gentle dawn of his presence in her heart.

— Sheila Cusack

INVITE MARY to your prayers one morning. Ask her to gently take your hand and to lead you to God.

Prayer: Mary, help me to quiet my heart today, so that I am able to listen to the gentle voice of the Lord speaking to me and to experience the dawn of his presence.

Friday After Ash Wednesday: Serenity

"Be still, and know I am God." — *Psalms 46:10*

Mary offers us an example on how to live in stillness with God. Through a quiet and humble life of prayer, Mary was able to contemplate on the workings of the Lord in her life. In spite of the difficulties and hardships that Mary encountered, her faith never wavered and she was able to remain calm and serene before the Lord God Almighty. Mary's serenity came from her act of spiritual surrender to God. Freely and without hesitation, Mary gave herself over to the Lord not only when asked to be the mother of Jesus but every day of her life.

As our heavenly mother, Mary invites us to follow her example. When we are stressed, fearful, or anxious, let us turn to our Blessed Mother for the reassurance we need to be still. Let us seek Mary's help to surrender these difficult events into the hands of the Lord, so that we may know that God is with us.

— Gina Sannasardo

HOW CAN THE KNOWLEDGE that God is with you bring serenity to your family life? Work life? Spiritual life? Ask Mary to help you be still today so that you can see God at work in your life.

Prayer: Blessed Mother, strengthen us so that we can experience God's presence all around us.

Saturday After Ash Wednesday: Generosity

"For by grace you have been saved through faith;
and this is not your own doing, it is the gift of God —
not because of works, lest any man should boast."
— Ephesians 2:8-9

How generous is our God! How great is the abundance of God's mercy and kindness. Our salvation is a gift of grace. We can't earn it. Therefore, we have nothing to brag about.

Mary was the recipient of God's enormous generosity. She was full of the grace of salvation because she opened her heart to fully receive all that God wanted to give her. She immersed herself in her mission as the mother of Jesus. Selflessly, she served not only as Jesus' mother but also as a faithful disciple of her Son in his mission of salvation. Mary shows us how to receive the generosity of God's love, mercy, and grace that await us.

— John Holmes

HOW CAN YOU RESPOND more fully to God's generosity today? Ask Mary to help you open your heart fully to receive God's gifts.

Prayer: Blessed Lady, thank you for your example of God's generosity. Help me to follow that I may find my true calling.

~ SELF-CONTROL ~

First Week of Lent, Sunday

"I can do all things in him who strengthens me."
— *Philippians 4:13*

As a person in recovery from emotional overeating, I know that self-control is very misunderstood. To most, self-control is pulling up your boot straps — a "super willpower," so to speak. That is not biblical. Each time we think that way and fail, we add to our belief that we can't control ourselves. Self-control is the fruit of living the life of Christ; it is he who gives us the strength to overcome our struggles.

Throughout the pages of Scripture, Mary continually demonstrated self-control. There were certainly times when she had to hold her tongue. Mary's ultimate act of self-control was not to rush in to try to save her Son from crucifixion or cry out with anger and bitterness at the betrayal he had suffered. Mary's self-control was the fruit of living a life of deep faith.

— Christine Grano

WHAT STRUGGLES HAVE YOU HAD with self-control? Write down how you feel about those struggles and spend time with that in prayer.

Prayer: Mary, thank you for your quiet exhibition of self-control. Pray for me that my mind may be renewed in the true source of self-control. Please pray that I open myself to be empowered by the Lord.

First Week of Lent, Monday

"Behold, your mother!" — *John 19:27*

Although I am a cradle Catholic, I didn't put much effort into my faith until I was thirty-five years old and a priest friend encouraged me to pray each day. Since prayer was not part of my life, I began slowly and said a few Our Fathers, Hail Marys, and Glory Bes as I walked to work. A few weeks later, I discovered that there was a noon Mass near my work. I also tried to pray the Rosary occasionally. Now, thirty years later, prayer has become my lifestyle. I attend daily Mass, read Scripture, sit in silent meditation, and pray the Rosary often.

Prayer has drawn me into an intimate relationship with Jesus through his mother, Mary. I believe that's why Jesus gave us his mother from the cross. Jesus knew that Mary would lead us to him.

Prayer, like any relationship, evolves over time and takes some self-control. You can't pray if you don't make a conscious effort. Mary understands the daily demands of our busy lives, and she knows it takes self-control on our part to focus our energy on prayer.

— Bob Frazee

TODAY, PRAY ONE HAIL MARY, one Our Father, and one Glory Be, or add a few minutes to your established prayer time.

Prayer: Mother Mary, guide me to your Son through a life of prayer.

First Week of Lent, Tuesday

"For what does it profit a man, to gain the whole world and forfeit his life?" — Mark 8:36

At the top of my list of indulgences are dark chocolate, a glass of wine, and traveling. You might wonder how something so small could be bad for you? Well, it doesn't hurt to have a few satisfying moments. It's when we *over*indulge or *self*-indulge that problems arise.

Losing self-control has taken me down the paths of gaining weight and prioritizing success over almost everything else. Failing to say "no" to myself even cost me contact with friends and compromised my relationship with God.

Mary reveals the power of saying "yes." She could have chosen to take a path that required less of her and brought her more immediate gratification. But, Mary's faith was strong. Practicing self-control, Mary chose Christ over the world, and over herself.

— Deb Kelsey-Davis

THINK OF YOUR OWN weaknesses. We all have them. Are there things in your life that just might be separating you from God?

Prayer: Mary, help me to take my temptations and turn those struggles over to God as you did. Show me how to practice self-control so that I more fully may know the love of the Father and choose Jesus.

First Week of Lent, Wednesday

*"Therefore gird up your minds, be sober, set your hope
fully upon the grace that is coming to you at the
revelation of Jesus Christ." — 1 Peter 1:13*

Mary's life invites us to prepare our minds and
fix our hope on the grace of God. Sinless from birth,
Mary still had to look evil in the eye and practice
self-control over temptations that came her way. As
sons and daughters of Christ, our spiritual mother is
here to help us keep sober and overcome all sin and
temptation.

Because Mary completely focused on Jesus, she
was able to say "no" to the things of this world even
when they seemed attractive or better. She delighted
in saying "yes" to the Lord's plan for her and extends
her hands to us so that we may join her in saying "yes"
to God.

— Gina Sannasardo

HOW CAN YOU PRACTICE self-control today? Ask Mary
to always stay with you so that in moments of weakness she can be your strength.

*Prayer: Beloved Mother, I come to you with hope and con-
fidence that you will protect me from the false values of this
world so that I may give myself totally to God.*

First Week of Lent, Thursday

"Then the righteous will shine like the sun in the kingdom of their Father. He who has ears, let him hear."
— Matthew 13:43

Mary was present with her Son, Jesus, through both light and darkness. She exemplified grace even during times of frustration and unexpected news. Drawing upon her strong faith in the Lord, Mary was able to exercise self-control when dealing with the miraculous events in her life — that is, situations that she encountered but did not understand. Mary never questioned God; rather she placed her complete trust in the ways of the Lord.

Mary can teach us how to deal with difficult situations and events in our lives that we don't fully understand. Instead of reacting in a negative way, we can follow Mary's example and prayerfully ponder things in our hearts as we give them over to the Lord. When we do, we will shine like the sun in the kingdom of our heavenly Father.

— Sheila Cusack

THINK OF A RELATIONSHIP or event in your life that could be improved if you practiced self-control. Seek the Blessed Mother's assistance in dealing with this situation.

Prayer: Mary, pray that I can exercise self-control in my dealings with people and events that are problematic for me.

First Week of Lent, Friday

"Be still, and know that I am God." — Psalm 46:10

At the Annunciation, Mary opened her life, her body, her soul to her God. She said "yes" to her beloved and gave God control over her life. Instead of trying to control him, or everything around her, Mary was content to control herself.

Can I trust that God's love will hold me when I need it most? That I can relinquish my (illusory) sense of control and count on his strength in place of mine? To learn from his wisdom? To hear his Word? Am I willing to be vulnerable, open, truly humble? How can I receive God's grace if I don't trust him?

We don't hear God in the hurricane in our minds. We don't feel God in the earthquake in our hearts. We don't learn from God in a life of distraction and fluttering. We hear God in stillness as a light murmuring sound or a "still small voice." We exercise the greatest self-control when we learn to rely fully on him.

— Jane Zimmerman

SIT STILL FOR FIVE MINUTES today. Listen to the noise that is within you, then ask Mary to help you learn to exercise genuine self-control and be still.

Prayer: Dear Mary, please help me to be still, so I can feel God's presence and store his treasures in my heart as you did.

First Week of Lent, Saturday

"And the angel said to her." — Luke 1:30

There is a beautiful painting entitled *The Angelus* by Jean-Francois Millet. It depicts a man and woman working in the fields pausing at dusk to pray. Their postures evoke a feeling of deep reverence. I like to imagine our Blessed Mother teaching Jesus the prayers and rituals a young Jewish boy would learn growing up. A holy, prayerful life requires a certain amount of effort, including discipline and self-control.

Mary models these traits as she surrenders to the message of the angel, observes the purification rituals, attends Passover, and quietly walks the Way of the Cross with Jesus. Mary made time in her life for God, and she invites us to do the same.

Several years ago, I set the alarm on my cell phone to quietly chime at noon and 6:00 p.m. Hearing that soft chime is like a tap on the shoulder reminding me it's time to be with God — and Mary.

— Bob Frazee

A MORNING OFFERING, an examination of conscience, grace before meals, daily Mass, and readings of the day are all ways of making time for God. Be creative and find what works for you.

Prayer: Mary, I pray to you for guidance. Show me the way to make time for God.

~ GENEROSITY ~

Second Week of Lent, Sunday

"The Pharisee stood and prayed thus with himself, 'God, I thank you that I am not like the other men, extortioners, unjust, adulterers, or even like this tax collector. I fast twice a week, I give tithes of all that I get.'" — Luke 18:11-12

The kind of generosity Scripture talks about is a fruit of our redemption, not a means to self-satisfaction. The Pharisee in this passage didn't talk about his generosity from a place of graced humility or as an outflow of the Spirit, but rather from a place of self-importance. We have all known people who give generously simply because they want to appear important to others. They seek affirmation for their good deeds.

Mary's life of humility reminds us that God looks at our hearts. We are called to give generously to others, but from a place of humble service to the Lord.

— Christine Grano

DO A HEART CHECK today — where does my generosity flow from? How can I be more generous to others in the name of Jesus?

Prayer: Mary, pray that I allow the Holy Spirit to continue the work of transformation in my life so that my generosity flows freely and from humble gratitude.

Second Week of Lent, Monday

"Now may the LORD *show mercy and faithfulness to you!
And I will do good to you because you have done
this thing." —* 2 Samuel 2:6

My sister is one of the most generous people I know. She gives her time, money, and, most importantly, love freely. She is constantly doing something kind; it comes very naturally to her.

Being generous is not always easy. Sometimes we want to store up and hold onto things, just in case. But that is not what God asks us to do. He wants us to trust him and know that he will be generous with us, because he loves us. Generosity flows from knowing that we are heirs to God's kingdom and are loved by a truly generous God.

Mary's "yes" to God was one of the most generous acts in human history. Through her generosity, God could be even more generous to us and give us the most precious gift of all — salvation in his Son, Jesus.

— Suzette Horyza

TODAY, LOOK FOR SIGNS of God's love for you. Consider giving something you'd rather keep to someone else.

Prayer: Mary, show me how much God loves me. And help me to model my life after yours by being generous in spirit.

Second Week of Lent, Tuesday

*"Honor the LORD with your substance, / and with
the first fruits of all your produce; / then your barns
will be filled with plenty, / and your vats will be
bursting with wine." — Proverbs 3:9-10*

Our family of second-generation Italians struggled
for years and depended on the generosity of people, in-
stitutions, and the government for assistance. As a result,
we sometimes overlooked the gifts God had given us.

Mary teaches us how to remain focused on God's
gifts. The chosen mother of our Savior, Mary em-
braced the overshadowing of the Holy Spirit. Later,
she was present when the Holy Spirit descended on
the disciples gathered at Pentecost. Mary generously
gave of herself all her life; first as the mother of Jesus,
and then as a mother to the small community of be-
lievers from which our faith grew.

Mary's example has helped me to recognize the
generous gifts that God has given me. I no longer
look for generosity from other people. Instead, I try to
respond to the needs of others out of love and gratitude to Jesus and his mother, Mary.

— Michael Grano

WHAT IS THE MOTIVATION for your generosity? Does it
depend on other people, or the gifts of the Holy Spirit?

*Prayer: Mary, please ask Jesus to help me to remember and
honor his gracious generosity present in my life.*

Second Week of Lent, Wednesday

"You shall remember the LORD your God, for it he who gives you power to get wealth." — *Deuteronomy 8:18*

Jewish faith supports the acquisition of wealth, but it comes with a condition. A portion of one's wealth must be shared with the needy and less fortunate. In following this practice, a person's acts of love for the poor also displayed love for God and a recognition of his generosity.

Mary and Joseph would have followed the laws regarding tithing. They would have given ten percent of what they earned to others, not because they had to, but because it was the right thing to do. The needs of the less fortunate were never an afterthought. Every day presented opportunities to share their blessings with others in need. We can choose to follow Mary's example of generosity, not because we have to, but because it is still the right thing to do.

— Sharon A. Abel, PhD

HOW CAN YOU DO MORE to respond to the needs of others? Make a plan. Start today.

Prayer: Mary, give me the grace to shoulder the responsibility to raise up the poor in our world. Because God has been generous to me, I have so much to give. Help me to remember that when I care for and love the needy, I also love Our Lord.

Second Week of Lent, Thursday

"Now the company of those who believed were of one heart and soul, and no one said that any of the things which he possessed was his own, but they had everything in common. There was not any one needy among them, for as many as were possessors of lands or houses sold them, and brought the proceeds of what was sold and laid it at the apostles' feet; and distribution was made to each as any had need." — Acts 4:32,34-35

This powerful passage from Acts reminds us that in the early Church those who followed the teachings of Jesus were of one heart and soul. They shared everything with one another. Even as the mother of Jesus, Mary would have shared whatever possessions she had with the followers of her Son.

Mary encourages us to be generous in giving. She inspires us to open our hearts and our spirits to the people among us, to share our belongings with those who have nothing, and to share our faith with those who hunger and thirst for God in their lives.

— Lauren Nelson

How can you be of service to your brothers and sisters in Christ today?

Prayer: Mary, we are all of one heart and soul in your Son. Help me to follow your example of generosity in giving to others.

Second Week of Lent, Friday

"Pray at all times in the Spirit, with all prayer and supplication. To that end keep alert with all perseverance, making supplication for all the saints." — *Ephesians 6:18*

Over my life, I have had many people ask me to pray for their needs; likewise, I have asked others to pray for me and my family. What always amazes me are the people who pray for me even when I don't ask.

Recently, I got a text from someone who told me that she had been praying for me. At Christmastime, another person gave me a baby quilt that she crocheted for my soon-to-be grandson and told me that she prayed for him with each stitch.

When we come to Mary with our prayer needs, her generosity overflows as she intercedes for us. She never stops praying for us. As a mother, Mary knows what we need and will pray to her Son on our behalf.
— Christine Grano

REFLECT UPON THOSE INDIVIDUALS in your life who have been generous with their prayers for you. Offer prayers for their needs.

Prayer: Mary, thank you for your generosity in praying for me. Please pray that I, too, will be generous in my prayers for those in need.

Second Week of Lent, Saturday

"He has filled the hungry with good things, / and the rich he has sent empty away. / He has helped his servant Israel, / in remembrance of his mercy." — Luke 1:53-54

While most of us will never know the pains of hunger that come from a lack of sufficient food, the reality of life is that we all hunger for something. Some of us hunger for justice and equality in the workplace; others hunger for peace. Some people hunger for happiness, while others are in search of love and companionship. Whatever we hunger for, Mary assures us that the Lord will remember us with mercy, and will generously fill the hungry with good things.

Mary's Magnificat prayer of praise challenges us to reassess our priorities. Do we seek more wealth and possessions? Are we the rich that will be sent away empty? Or are we content with the blessings God has generously given us?

— Dr. Mary Amore

WHAT DO YOU HUNGER FOR in life? How can you refocus your priorities to seek the things of heaven instead of the things on earth? Seek Mary's help in desiring only those things in life that will lead us closer to the Lord.

Prayer: Mary, you generously gave of yourself to the Lord. Help me to hunger for the good things in life that will lead me to the heart of your Son, Jesus.

~ SERENITY ~

Third Week of Lent, Sunday

"Cast your burden on the LORD, / and he will sustain you; / he will never permit / the righteous to be moved."
— Psalms 55:22

The psalmist assures us that when we totally surrender to the Father's will, everything will work according to God's will. Mary believed this with all her heart and invites us to live in this sacred place of knowing that God is all we need. The Lord will never leave us alone, nor will he ever forget us. Jesus gave Mary to us as a heavenly mother because he knows we need to be nurtured, protected, and cared for.

On earth, Mary trusted in the Lord's plan for her and cast her fears aside, calmly awaiting guidance for her life without fear or anxiety. In heaven, with perfection and grace, Mary is seeking to help us obtain the favors we ask of the Lord.

— Gina Sannasardo

HOW CAN YOU QUIETLY WAIT for God's call and message to live your life? Ask Mary to sit patiently with you so that no fear may arise.

Prayer: Blessed Mother, I humbly ask that you provide me the strength to let go and let God. Help me to find rest and serenity in Christ so that I, too, may not fall.

Third Week of Lent, Monday

"Let not your hearts be troubled, neither let them be afraid." — John 14:27

Mary is often referred to as the Queen of Peace. Although Mary knew difficulty and experienced tremendous tragedy, she never lost serenity because she loved and trusted in the Lord.

It is very easy for us to have peace when everything is going our way. But the peace that Jesus brings to us is different from what the world can bring. His is a serenity that surpasses all our understanding. It enables us to find peace in our souls even when life is burdensome.

Mary chose to live in God's security each day. As our heavenly mother, Mary invites us to follow her example and trust in the Lord on a daily basis. If we give our concerns and all our needs to Jesus the way Mary did, he will help us find the pathway to serenity. Mary is there to help us walk that path.

— Deborah O'Donnell

WHAT CAN YOU DO to find serenity in your daily life? How might you share that gift with others?

Prayer: Mary, let peace come into my mind, body, and soul. Let me walk in your footsteps of peace and serenity.

Third Week of Lent, Tuesday

"Have no anxiety about anything, but in everything by prayer and supplication with thanksgiving let your requests be made known to God." — Philippians 4:6

The Bible often advises us to bring our needs and worries to God. Some days it is difficult for us to let go of our worries and offer our needs in prayer. From personal experience, I know how easy it can be to allow daily distractions and an over-connected culture steal my calm and push prayer time further down my list of priorities.

In Mary, we have a mother who can gently lead us to a renewed prayer life that will restore peace and serenity to our hectic lives. It was Mary who taught her Son, Jesus, to pray to the God of Abraham and Isaac. Mary can show us, too, how to lay our worries and needs before God.

— Deb Kelsey-Davis

INVITE MARY TO GUIDE YOU in prayer, to meditate upon God's love in your life. Ask Mary to bring your needs to her Son and help you find serenity.

Prayer: Mary, open my heart to the serenity that comes from prayer, that I might truly let go of my worries and trust in your Son, Jesus.

Third Week of Lent, Wednesday

"The LORD said to him, 'Peace be to you; do not fear.'"
— *Judges 6:23*

We tend to think that the ancient world in which Mary lived was stress-free and less hectic than our current world. But Nazareth would have been a crowded and busy town. Tradesmen and officials would be up early tending their businesses. The market and square would be bustling with social announcements, gatherings, merchants, and animals. Women would travel back and forth to the town well for water as needed. Their days were spent preparing meals, baking bread, cleaning homes, mending garments, and watching children. There wasn't much time for recreation or leisure.

Life's struggles of that time certainly fed fears and accentuated anxieties; Mary was not spared from them. Still, her faith in God kept her calm and drove her fears away. Mary seeks to help us de-stress our lives and restore serenity within us. We can turn to the Blessed Mother for help when we are fearful, and for hope when we despair.

— Sharon A. Abel, PhD

FEELING ANY STRESS TODAY? Ask Mary to walk with you as you seek to restore balance and serenity.

Prayer: Mary, grace me with your calm and serene temperament during stressful times. Help me to remember that the Lord never abandons me, that he is always near.

Third Week of Lent, Thursday

"Trust in the LORD with all your heart, / and do not rely on your own insight. / In all your ways acknowledge him, / and he will make straight your paths." — Proverbs 3:5-6

We all encounter difficult people and circumstances. Sometimes we are able to respond calmly, remain content, and be present. Other times we react violently, grow angry, and become distracted. Overwhelmed, we can feel pulled in many directions, even torn apart.

Jesus would tell us, "Don't be afraid"; and Mary would help us recognize that we make ourselves upset over circumstances outside ourselves, worried over things we cannot control, frustrated by situations we cannot change. Mary would encourage us to let go of the belief that we can fix everything or make things better by rehashing them. Mary would remind us that trusting just in our own efforts is ineffective. She would encourage us to stay on the path — that is, keep goodness in our minds, hold love in our hearts, and act and speak with integrity. Mary would instruct us that we are not called to be perfect, but whole.

— Jane Zimmerman

THE WHOLE PERSON acknowledges both light and dark and trusts God's grace to transform all things in Christ. Focus on that.

Prayer: Mary, please nudge me when I am being pulled away from God's grace — and remind me to stay on the path and trust in God.

Third Week of Lent, Friday

"He has showed you, O man, what is good; / and what does the LORD require of you / but to do justice, and to love kindness, / and to walk humbly with your God?"
— *Micah 6:8*

Not knowing all the details, or wanting to know the why and how of things, steals my serenity more than I care to admit. I have struggled at times with wanting to know God's plan for me and then trying to figure out how to carry it out. It's exhausting.

Mary's spirit is serenely calm. Her life inspires me to let go of details that can destroy my inner peace and to refocus my attention to trusting in the Lord. Mary did not know God's whole plan for her, but she trusted him. Her faith-filled heart allowed her to step back without worry and to let him handle every situation. Mary's life reminds us that if we desire serenity, all that is required of us is to trust in the Lord, to do what he commands, and to walk humbly with God.

— Deb Kelsey-Davis

HAVE YOU HAD MOMENTS of doubt or anxiety about turning your problems over to the Lord? How might Mary's example illuminate a path of peace and serenity in letting go?

Prayer: Mary, fill my heart with the same faith you have in order that I might step aside and let Jesus guide me in all matters.

Third Week of Lent, Saturday

"To him who conquers I will grant to eat of the tree of life, which is in the paradise of God." — Revelation 2:7

There's a beautiful Japanese Garden in Chicago named Sansho-En, lush with bonsai trees, evergreens, flowers, and limestone pathways. Basins of water are placed throughout the garden in special locations to allow visitors to purify themselves, both physically (by washing their hands and drinking water) and spiritually (by symbolically washing away one's cares). Sansho-En's design was intended to present natural serenity.

For me, Mary's life exemplifies a natural serenity — a serenity that is real, tangible, and human. Our Blessed Mother's tranquility stems from her close relationship with God. As our spiritual mother, Mary hopes that all of her children will draw near to the Lord so that we, too, may experience serenity as our natural state. We were created to be at peace with God and one another; this is not something extraordinary and elusive but is within reach.

— Joseph Abel, PhD

FIND A DESIGNATED WALKING PATH in a nearby park, garden, or hiking trail. Spend time walking on the path or trail. Invite God to walk with you. Allow beauty and natural serenity to fill your heart.

Prayer: Mary, help me to discover the serenity that comes from being one with God. Take my hand and lead me to the path where God awaits me.

~ GENTLENESS ~

Fourth Week of Lent, Sunday

"With all lowliness and meekness, with patience, forbearing one another in love, eager to maintain the unity of the Spirit in the bond of peace." — *Ephesians 4:2-3*

Life can be chaotic at times. Frustrating or challenging moments in relationships with family, friends, and associates can make it difficult to remain gentle in our expressions and behaviors. Impulse can take over, and we may want to "speak our minds" rather than "hold our tongues." It is in these occasions that we need to stop, reflect, and invite Mary to be present with us. When we call on her to help us redirect our behaviors, and reflect what is good and pleasing to God, we open ourselves to the graces which are meant for us.

Imagine the gentleness, patience, and love that Mary demonstrated, not only in accepting the call to be the mother of God, but also in witnessing her son's mission on earth.

— Nanci Lukasik-Smith

How CAN YOU TAKE Mary's example of gentleness and patience to heart today? During your most difficult moments, is there a way you can demonstrate gentleness so that others can witness Christ working through you?

Prayer: Mary, please remind me when I am challenged and distracted. Redirect my thoughts and actions to imitate the gentle, loving nature of Christ so I can reflect his holy mission.

Fourth Week of Lent, Monday

"He will feed his flock like a shepherd, / he will gather the lambs in his arms, / he will carry them in his bosom, / and gently lead those that are with young."
— *Isaiah 40:11*

For centuries, master artists have depicted Jesus as the gentle shepherd carrying the lost sheep. Upon prayerful reflection, we can imagine that Jesus may well have learned gentleness from his mother, Mary. Each day of his life, Mary taught Jesus how to be kind, gentle, and compassionate, as any good mother would do.

When we pray the Hail Mary, the words of this heartfelt prayer remind us that the Lord is with Mary. If we follow her example in life, the Lord will be with us as well. Mary and Jesus are here to tend to our spiritual needs and to carry us home to heaven in their loving arms. May the prayer of our hearts reflect this beautiful spiritual reality.

— Sheila Cusack

CALL TO MIND a difficult situation you are going through. Invite Mary to bring you to the Good Shepherd, that you may not be lost, but cradled and carried by the Lord through difficulty.

Prayer: Mary, help us to hear the voice of your Son, Jesus, the Good Shepherd, that we may never stray from his flock.

Fourth Week of Lent, Tuesday

"Aim at righteousness, godliness, faith, love, steadfastness, gentleness." — 1 Timothy 6:11

A homeless man entered my parish church to warm himself. He walked down the center aisle, removed his hat, and gazed at the cross in the sanctuary. He then ambled toward where I was standing — the back corner by a statue of Mary.

The beautiful, life-sized sculpture depicts the Annunciation. Mary has just said "yes" to God. Her hands, face, and eyes are raised toward the heavens in a gentle moment of chosen surrender.

For some time, the man gazed into Mary's eyes. He reverently touched her outreached hand, the hem of her garment, and her foot. Then, he asked me, "Who is this woman?" I responded: "Her name is Mary. She's the mother of Jesus."

He replied: "Her eyes are so gentle and full of love. She reminds me of my mother, who died when I was a boy. No one has looked at me like that for a long time. May I come visit her again?"

I responded, "Any time, sir." He left the church with a broad smile and returned to visit Mary often to receive the gentleness he saw in her.

— Sharon A. Abel, PhD

CONSIDER THE WAYS you can greet with gentleness the next stranger you meet.

Prayer: Mary, help me to be a kind, gentle, and loving person all the days of my life.

Fourth Week of Lent, Wednesday

*"Let all men know your forbearance [gentleness].
The Lord is at hand." — Philippians 4:5*

Most people think of a gentle person as some-one who is kind, but weak. In reality, a gentle person is strong. It takes strength to offer a gentle smile, a soothing word, or a helping hand, to treat everyone with kindness, to forgive, and to be faithful. This is how Mary lived.

Throughout her life, Mary exemplified gentleness through many difficult situations: when the angel Gabriel announced God's plan for her, even though she was terrified; when she and Joseph made the difficult journey to Bethlehem at the end of her pregnancy; as she gave birth to Jesus in a stable; with the child Jesus, even when she did not understand his words or his actions; at the wedding in Cana, when she quietly urged Jesus to perform his first miracle; as she stood at the foot of the cross watching her son die in agony; and in the Upper Room praying with the disciples at Pentecost.

— Mary Kostic

AS WE THINK about the world we live in today, we can choose to return to the strength of gentleness and treat everyone with kindness, compassion, and love.

Prayer: Mary, help us to grow in gentleness by your example and through your Son, Jesus. Help us find the strength to be compassionate, kind, and patient.

Fourth Week of Lent, Thursday

"A soft answer turns away wrath, / but a harsh word stirs up anger." — Proverbs 15:1

Do you have a family member or friend who is soft-spoken and gentle in their mannerisms? I do. Actually, I have several who qualify with these characteristics. They are firm in their faith, yet they can engage others in a warm and respectful approach. Even with heavy or controversial subjects they come across as calm and confident. They provide a genuine softness that makes one feel at ease, and the conversation is positive for all involved.

I imagine that our Blessed Mother was like this in her dealings with people. Her gentle nature and respectful demeanor helped others to know and love Jesus. Mary's life inspires us to listen to others with respect.

— Nanci Lukasik-Smith

CONSIDER THE WAYS you can exhibit a gentle nature, one of welcome and warmth. What could you do today to make others feel comfortable in your presence?

Prayer: Holy Mary, when I am with others, please help me to represent the kind of character that is pleasing to the Father. Let me be welcoming and gentle in bringing others to Christ. Guide me to speak and act in ways that draw people to your Son.

Fourth Week of Lent, Friday

"The LORD is gracious and merciful, / slow to anger and abounding in mercy." — *Psalm 145:8*

Mary is a model of goodness, love, and grace. This is most evident in the early days of Mary's role as the mother of Jesus. As a new mother, Mary was gracious in welcoming the shepherds who came to see her newborn baby boy. She opened her heart to foreigners, too — the Magi from the East who brought gifts. From the moment of his birth, Mary realized that she would have to share Jesus with all those who would seek him.

Mary's life has much to teach us about how to bring gentleness to today's world. So much of our culture seems to relish turmoil. People are quick to argue, and many judge and condemn others simply because they see things differently. Our heavenly mother invites us to graciously welcome the stranger, for we are all children of our heavenly Father.

— Lauren Nelson

REACH OUT TO SOMEONE today, perhaps someone you don't understand well, and encourage that person with gentle and compassionate words.

Prayer: Mary, your heart is gentle and pure. Help me to be welcoming and act with gentleness toward all people.

Fourth Week of Lent, Saturday

"My mouth will tell of your righteous acts, / of your deeds of salvation all the day, / for their number is past my knowledge." — Psalms 71:15

This Scripture passage challenges us to use our words to proclaim the goodness of God. Sadly, however, we often fall to the temptation to become caught up in a whirlwind of verbal conflict. At times, we may even tear down another person just to prove our point.

Actions speak even more clearly and eloquently. When we choose gentleness over power and control, our actions proclaim God's love. No one is a better example of that life-giving choice than Mary. As our heavenly mother, Mary is here to accompany us on our paths of conflict. She invites us to cultivate gentleness in all our relationships, even when we see our circumstances only through the cloudy lens of strife and division. When this happens, we can seek her assistance.

— Sheila Cusack

PRAYERFULLY CALL TO MIND a recent disagreement or argument you had with another person. Invite Mary's gentle presence to help you walk away from this strife and disagreement, choose gentleness, and seek reconciliation.

Prayer: Mary, help me remember your Son's strife on earth. Help me to know that the conflicts I experience are opportunities to grow in gentleness.

~ SURRENDER ~

Fifth Week of Lent, Sunday

"When the feast was ended, as they were returning, the boy Jesus stayed behind in Jerusalem. His parents did not know it." — Luke 2:43

Where was Jesus? Mary wondered and worried for three days as she and Joseph wandered in search of their twelve-year-old son. The distress Mary felt shows in her words: "Son, why have you treated us so? Behold, your father and I have been looking for you anxiously" (Lk 2:48).

Like Mary, we can be overwrought in the face of unknowing, ambiguity, and distress. For most of us, being thrust into the unknown, the space of uncertainty, is difficult and frightening. As a human being, Mary must certainly have experienced the feelings of upset, worry, and distress when Jesus was missing. That shared human experience is why Mary can hear our prayers compassionately. But Mary knew that even in the unknown God was with her. That reality gave her the courage to surrender to him.

— Dr. Barb Jarvis Pauls

WHAT ARE YOU ANXIOUS or distressed about today? What are the uncertainties you are facing in your life? Ask Mary to help you find Jesus in the midst of them.

Prayer: Holy Mary, help us surrender with faith and trust in God's presence, even when we lose sight of him.

Fifth Week of Lent, Monday

"And he called to him the multitude with his disciples, and said to them, 'If any man would come after me, let him deny himself and take up his cross and follow me. For whoever would save his life will lose it; and whoever loses his life for my sake and the gospel's will save it.'"
— Mark 8:34-35

To those of us who want to follow Christ, the challenge is clear. Denying ourselves and taking up our crosses is an act of surrender. We surrender our desire for security, affection, and most of all control. We surrender those ego drivers we think are so important. Mary did this from the outset. She surrendered in perfect trust to God's will for her.

When our crosses seem more than we can bear, we can turn to Mother Mary, who can help us find the courage to surrender our lives to God. When we surrender our crosses, we gain the strength to carry them, and gain a better perspective on bearing the trials in our lives.

— John Holmes

WHAT CROSS ARE YOU CARRYING at the moment? Ask Mary's help in placing this matter into the hands of our loving Lord.

Prayer: Holy Mother, thank you for your example of trusting in the Lord. Help me to surrender all that I have in the hopes of gaining eternal life.

Fifth Week of Lent, Tuesday

"Be still, and know that I am God." — Psalms 46:10

My husband and I often spend time at a lake in northern Wisconsin. At dusk, once the fishermen retire, the lake becomes quiet and still. We like to drift with the current on a pontoon boat and watch magnificent sunsets. This is followed by a clear view of a breathtaking night sky which features billions of stars. There the breadth and depth of God's creation is set before us. With minds free from distractions, we are ready to embrace the silence and totally surrender to God's loving presence.

Total surrender to God means that we, like Mary, accept that we are not in control of what God may call us to do. Mary's life invites us to trust in God's providence, to let go and allow our creator God to work within us. We are his, and God has a plan for us. Stillness and silence invites God to lead. When we finally surrender our lives to God, we will come fully alive.

— Sharon A. Abel, PhD

TAKE TIME TODAY to be still. Surrender to the presence of the Lord. Listen for what God is speaking to you. May your response be, "Lead me, Lord."

Prayer: Mary, you have taught me how to be still before the Lord. You listened, God spoke, and his plan for our salvation fell into place. May I listen, and surrender, to God's plan for me.

Fifth Week of Lent, Wednesday

"Come to me, all who labor and are heavy laden, and I will give you rest." — *Matthew 11:28*

Here, the Lord is asking us to surrender our problems into his loving care. He wants us to let go of our desire to control the people and events of our life and trust in him. This is a difficult task for many people.

Mary's life shows us the pathway to spiritual surrender. As the mother of our Savior, Mary lovingly let go of Jesus when it came time for him to leave her and follow his call to preach, heal, and evangelize. She also surrendered the unspeakable pain of her broken heart as she stood beneath the cross as Jesus gave his life so that we could live with him forever.

So much of what we experience every day can be lifted off of our shoulders simply by giving it to the Lord. We can follow Mary's example and prayerfully surrender our joys and sorrows to the Lord and find rest in his loving arms.

— Dr. Barb Jarvis Pauls

WHAT BURDENS CAN I HAND OVER to the Lord this day? What joys can I give to God?

Prayer: Mother Mary, help me to trust in the workings of the Lord, that I may have the strength to surrender both the problems and joys of my life into the hands of our loving God.

Fifth Week of Lent, Thursday

"Behold, I am the handmaid of the Lord; let it be to me according to your word." — Luke 1:38

From a worldly perspective, surrender can seem a lot like weakness. Whenever someone is giving up, we tend to see it as a failure. But surrendering to God is a completely different experience. It is anything but weakness and failure.

We see that Mary's visit with the angel Gabriel begins with fear and concern. But because Mary had already resolved to be the handmaid of the Lord, she surrenders to God's will. What comes from this surrender is nothing short of miraculous.

Surrendering to God is not an act of weakness. In fact, it is one of the most courageous things we can do. The world's message is to depend on ourselves; but God's continual message is to fear not and trust him. When we surrender our lives to the Lord, we can fully live in God's peace and joy. Our lives are transformed when we surrender to God.

— Suzette Horyza

THINK OF SOMETHING you once surrendered to God. What did God do with what you entrusted to him?

Prayer: Mary, teach me how to surrender the things in my life, especially those I cannot change; help me to follow in your footsteps by doing the will of God.

Fifth Week of Lent, Friday

*"You call me Teacher and Lord; and you are right, for so
I am. If I then, your Lord and Teacher, have washed your
feet, you also ought to wash one another's feet."*
— *John 13:13-14*

Jesus surrenders in action. He recognizes his relationship with his disciples but steps out of the role of Lord and teacher to one of servant. This very humble act is an image of surrender.

Mary was always the humble servant; often, simply by being present. She never made things about herself, but always about others, and always focused on Jesus. From the Annunciation to the wedding in Cana to her presence at the foot of her Son's cross, Mary was there as a servant. She was always prepared to surrender herself for others.

— John Holmes

How CAN YOU put yourself in service to others?

*Prayer: Mother Mary, thank you for your service and your
example of service in community. Help me to follow you and
your Son in the same way.*

Fifth Week of Lent, Saturday

"Behold, like the clay in the potter's hand, so are you in my hand, O house of Israel." — Jeremiah 18:6

Mary is the perfect example of clay in the hands of the potter. Mary allowed God to shape and form her life into what God desired her to be. She trusted that the Lord would gently mold her to perfection.

Even as her beloved Son hung on the cross, Mary accepted whatever she encountered as another movement of the potter's hands. She trusted that, just as the potter reveals the beauty of his creations, the beauty of her life would be revealed in God's handiwork.

We, too, are clay in the hands of our divine potter, and we are being shaped and molded by God. In this divine process of creation, we are invited to bend to God's will as the Lord makes of us what he intends. In the end, the beauty of our lives as fashioned by the hands of our creator will be revealed, just as it was in Mary's life.

— Lauren Nelson

How is the Lord fashioning your life? In what ways can you surrender to the creative forces of God?

Prayer: Mary, your life inspires me to be a moldable piece of clay in the hands of Our Lord. Guide me in surrendering my life to God, that I may become his divine creation. Amen.

~ FAITHFULNESS ~

Holy Week, Palm or Passion Sunday

"So they took branches of palm trees and went out to meet him, crying, 'Hosanna! Blessed is he who comes in the name of the Lord, even the King of Israel!'"
— John 12:13

None of us has any idea of what tomorrow will bring. Joy can turn into sorrow in the blink of an eye. On Palm Sunday, Mary's Son was hailed as King and palm branches paved a peaceful path for Jesus to enter into the city of Jerusalem. Not five days later, he was violently executed on a cross. While we may never know what Mary was feeling on Palm Sunday, we can be certain that it was her unwavering faith that sustained her in the days that followed.

Mary's life teaches us that our faith must be strong so that we can endure all that life will bring. She is here to help us deepen our faith in times of joy, so that we can find strength in times of suffering.

— Dr. Mary Amore

TAKE A MOMENT to thank the Lord for all of your blessings. Make a list of three joys that you can look to for strength when life is difficult.

Prayer: Mary, help me to deepen my relationship with Jesus so that I may have the strength and courage to carry my crosses from death to new life.

Holy Week, Monday

*"The LORD is my light and my salvation; /
whom shall I fear?"* — *Psalm 27:1*

After hearing about Jesus' triumphant entrance into Jerusalem, most assuredly Mary also heard the cries of the mob which were turning against her Son, calling him a blasphemer and seeking to stone him to death. In those last days, Mary found herself unable to protect her Son from the power of those who were seeking to harm him. Rather than fearing what was about to transpire, our Blessed Mother entrusted everything to the Lord.

Like Mary, we have moments in our lives that make us feel powerless. Perhaps a loved one is suffering and it becomes painful to accompany him or her through daily struggles. Perhaps a family member has turned away from God and we feel utterly helpless to change the situation. In moments of fear and anxiety, we can turn to Mother Mary and ask for help to deepen our faith in God and his presence in our lives.

— Dr. Mary Amore

INVITE MARY TO HELP you calm your fears and place your life completely in the hands of the Lord.

Prayer: Mary, help me increase my faith so that I may not fear the events of my life but recognize that the Lord is my light and my salvation.

Holy Week, Tuesday

"When it was evening, he sat at table with the twelve disciples; and as they were eating, he said, 'Truly, I say to you, one of you will betray me.'" — *Matthew 26:20-21*

The events leading to the passion and death of Jesus include many acts of betrayal. Among the worst were those of Judas Iscariot, one of the Twelve, who turned Jesus over to his enemies for thirty pieces of silver. These deeds of deception pierced Mary's heart with sorrow; yet Mary remained strong in her faith. She did not allow hurt to affect her relationship with God.

We, too, experience disappointment and hurt at the hands of those we love and trust. When a family member, spouse, or close friend betrays us, it can tear our hearts in two and fill us with a desire for revenge. Mary can help us turn away from the inclination to strike back. Her motherly love shows us how to regain our footing and trust God to take care of us when we are wronged.

— Dr. Mary Amore

CALL TO MIND a time when you felt betrayed. Ask Mary for the strength and guidance to pray for all those who have hurt you.

Prayer: Mary, your faith sustained you through many difficult times and kept you from seeking revenge. Help me to follow your example.

Holy Week, Wednesday

"He said to his disciples, 'You know that after two days the Passover is coming, and the Son of man will be delivered up to be crucified.'" — Matthew 26:1-2

What must have been going through Mary's mind as Jesus announced to his disciples that he was about to die? As his mother, her first instinct may have been to save Jesus from this horrible execution. Or perhaps she was tempted to get angry at God for what was about to transpire. Nevertheless, in the midst of unspeakable violence against her Son, Mary remained faithful to the Lord. She trusted that God would not abandon her — or Jesus — in their time of need.

Mary's experience as the mother of Jesus invites us to do some soul searching. When our lives are difficult and pain is everywhere, many of us tend to blame God for our troubles. We may even question our faith at its most basic level and ask, "Where are you, God?" Mary's life invites us to remain faithful in times of suffering — for God is with us always.

— Dr. Mary Amore

INVITE MARY TO FACE today's trials and tribulations with you.

Prayer: Mary, help me to follow your example and to place my pain and distress into the hands of the Lord.

Holy Week, Holy Thursday

"For I have given you an example, that you also should do as I have done to you." — John 13:15

At the Last Supper Jesus washed the feet of the disciples, providing them, and us, an example of humility and loving service. Humble service to others is not common in today's self-centered society as many people do favors for another with the expectation of receiving something in return. Genuine and selfless service is, however, the hallmark of a life of faithful discipleship. Jesus summons us to do for others as he has done for us.

No one demonstrates this better than Mary. Even as the hour of his death approached, Mary's life modeled a faithful response to the Lord's call to humble service. From the cradle to the cross, Mary never wavered in her faith. She lived her life as a humble handmaid of the Lord. Mary is here to help us recognize and lovingly respond to the needs of those in our life, without expecting anything in return.

— Dr. Mary Amore

CALL TO MIND a family member or friend who is in need. How can you serve that person today?

Prayer: Mother, your life is one of gentle service to the Lord. Help me to model my life after yours.

Holy Week, Good Friday

*"When Jesus saw his mother, and the disciple whom he
loved standing near, he said to his mother, 'Woman,
behold, your son!' Then he said to the disciple, 'Behold,
your mother!'" — John 19:26-27*

Mary's deep faith in God did not spare her from
suffering. Rather, it brought her to the foot of the
cross where she witnessed the brutal crucifixion and
death of her beloved Son, Jesus. As he hung there in
agony, Jesus did not abandon Mary, but entrusted his
mother to the care of his beloved disciple. In that moment, Mary became the mother of that disciple. She
also became the mother of all the disciples of Christ
in every place and age.

We have all suffered loss, and the deep wounds of
grief, anger, guilt, and despair can hinder our spiritual
growth. As our heavenly mother, Mary is here to hold
us in our darkest moments of grief and sorrow as only
a mother can. She is faithful in helping to tend our
spiritual wounds.

— Dr. Mary Amore

IS THERE A LOSS IN LIFE you are grieving? Ask Mary
to grieve with you and guide you on the path of ac-
ceptance and faith.

*Prayer: Mother of Mercy, take my hand and lead me through
the difficulties of this day.*

Holy Week, Holy Saturday

"[The women] saw the tomb, and how his body was laid;
then they returned, and prepared spices and ointments.
'On the Sabbath they rested according to the
commandment.'" — Luke 23:55-56

There is an ancient homily that speaks of the day immediately following the Crucifixion: "Today there is a great silence over the earth, a great silence, and stillness, a great silence because the King sleeps."

Those of us who have lost a loved one know this feeling, the great silence that comes over us; the feeling of a loss so deep that it echoes no sound within us.

Mary surely experienced this kind of profound silence at the death of Jesus. Yet her faith in the Lord did not fail. Faithfulness carried her, and all the women who mourned the loss of Jesus, through their sorrow. Though overwhelmed by sadness, the women prepared what would be needed to bury Jesus properly, and they rested as the law required them to do. They found the strength to remain faithful because they trusted that God would be faithful, too.

— Dr. Mary Amore

INVITE THE BLESSED MOTHER into your silence. Ask her to show you how to respond to loss with faith.

Prayer: Virgin most sorrowful, help me to live faithfully in the midst of loss and despair.

Holy Week, Easter Sunday

"Why do you seek the living among the dead?
He is not here, but has risen." — Luke 24:5

The Scriptures are filled with stories of Jesus appearing to various disciples after his resurrection, yet there is not a single account that speaks of him appearing to his mother, Mary. Early Christian tradition, however, has suggested an encounter between Mary and the risen Jesus. Perhaps that is why she was not at the tomb with the other women who went to anoint his body. Whatever the case, Mary's heart must have filled with joy and glory on that first Easter morning. Her faith was not in vain.

Today, so many of us are stuck in Good Friday moments of pain, fear, and despair. In our broken world, it is difficult for us to remain faithful and find hope in the midst of darkness. Mary's life invites us to trust in the Lord, so that he can transform our darkness into the glorious light of the Resurrection.

— Dr. Mary Amore

HAVE YOU BEEN SEEKING LIFE "among the dead"? Spend a few minutes asking Mary to help you find the risen Lord in your life today.

Prayer: Mary, your unwavering faith in the Lord inspires me. Help me to live my life in faithfulness with the hope and joy of the Risen Christ.

Dr. Mary Amore holds a Doctor of Ministry Degree in Liturgical Studies and a Master of Arts in Pastoral Studies. A published author and national presenter, Dr. Amore is the host of the television show *Soul Snackin' with Dr. Mary Amore* sponsored by Mayslake Ministries and is the full-time executive director of Mayslake Ministries.

Also edited by Dr. Mary Amore:

EVERY DAY WITH MARY

Your deeper and more personal relationship with the Blessed Mother can start today with the help of **Every Day with Mary**. Every day of the year you'll ponder the fruits of the Holy Spirit in Mary's life with a timely and relevant meditation perfect for your busy life. This daily devotional is sure to touch your heart, nourish your soul, and lead you to a deeper relationship with Christ through the intercession of his mother. **Inventory No. T1867**.

To order:
(800) 348-2440 or OSVCatholicBookstore.com